THE ALCHEMIST (COELHO)

Paulo Coelho

AUTHORED by Anthony P. Arroyo
UPDATED AND REVISED by Damien Chazelle

COVER DESIGN by Table XI Partners LLC
COVER PHOTO by Olivia Verma and © 2005 GradeSaver, LLC

BOOK DESIGN by Table XI Partners LLC

Published by GradeSaver LLC, www.gradesaver.com

First published in the United States of America by GradeSaver LLC. 2008

GRADESAVER, the GradeSaver logo and the phrase "Getting you the grade since 1999" are registered trademarks of GradeSaver, LLC

ISBN 978-1-60259-166-0

Printed in the United States of America

For other products and additional information please visit
http://www.gradesaver.com

Table of Contents

Table of Contents

Biography of Coelho, Paulo (1947-)

Paulo Coelho was born in Rio de Janeiro, Brazil on August 24, 1947. Before becoming the most widely published Brazilian author of all time–publishing close to 100 million books–he worked as a theatre director, an actor and a journalist. In the 1970's, Coelho was also a successful songwriter whose songs were sung by such well-known brazilian singers as Elis Regina, Rita Lee and, most notably, Brazilian psychadelic rock pioneer Raul Seixas. Seixas and Coelho recieved wide commercial and critical acclaim for their songs "Eu Nasci Há Dez Mil Anos Atrás," "Gita," "Al Capone" as well as 60 other songs. Also during this time, Coelho travelled the world as part of the hippy movement and became more and more interested in Eastern religions as well as occultism in general.

Coelho's definitive spiritual turn, however, came when he made a pilgrimage along the Camino de Santiago de Compostela, a catholic pilgrimage route in the north-western Spanish state of Galicia. This journey is documented in his book, *The Pilgrimage (O Diário de um Mago)*, released in 1988. His next book was *The Alchemist (O Alquimista)*, a book which he claims is a metaphorical adaptation of his own spiritual journey that he undertook on his pilgrimage. Clearly, the name of the protagonist in *The Alchemist* is a nod to Coelho's experience on the Camino de Santiago. While sales of *The Alchemist* were slow at first, it went on to become the highest-selling Brazilian book of all time and one of the most widely read books in the world.

Since publishing *The Alchemist*, Coelho has gone on to publish other titles including *Brida (1990), The Valkyries (As Valkírias, 1992), By the river Piedra I sat Down and Wept (Na margem do rio Piedra eu sentei e chorei, 1994), The Fifth Mountain (O Monte Cinco, 1996), Manual of a Warrior of Light (O Manual do Guerreiro da Luz, 1997), Veronika decides to die (Veronika decide morrer, 1998), The Devil and Miss Prym, (O demônio e a Srta. Prym, 2000), Eleven Minutes (Onze Minutos, 2003), The Zahir (O Zahir, 2005), The Witch of Portobello (A Bruxa de Portobello, 2006)* and, most recently, *The Winner Stands Alone (O Vencedor Está Só, 2008)*. In addition to his books, Coelho also has a weekly column which is published in several Brazilian newspapers and is syndicated internationally.

Coelho is not only an internationally acclaimed author, but is also an outspoken activist for peace and social justice. He is a Messenger of Peace for the UN, an Ambassador to the European Union for Intercultural Dialogue, a Member of the Board of the Shimon Peres Institute for Peace, a UNESCO Special Counselor for "Intercultural Dialogues and Spiritual Convergences," and a Board Member of the Schwab Foundation for Social Entrepreneurship. He is also a member of the Brazilian Academy of Letters, the highest honor for a Brazilian author, and is one of the best-known authors to actively support the free distribution of his work.

Paulo Coelho and his wife Christina split their time between Rio de Janeiro, Brazil and Saint Martin, Hautes-Pyrénées, France.

About The Alchemist (Coelho)

The Alchemist is one of the most important literary phenomenons of the 20th century, selling more than 30 million copies worldwide. The book has been translated into over 67 languages and tops the all-time best-seller list in 18 countries. The overwhelming success of *The Alchemist* can be ascribed to a few different things. First, the story of Santiago the shepherd is one of everyday spirituality, the kind of spirituality that people can use in their day-to-day lives. One of the central messages of the book is that spirituality is not something separate from an individual's need to realize his/her dreams. In fact, the things that one's heart truly desires are in fact messages from the universe. It is in pursuing these things to the best of one's ability that one is most truly alive. Second, *The Alchemist* is written in a straightforward style that allows its simple beauty to shine through. In this way, *The Alchemist* participates in a long tradition of religious and morality stories, such as fairy tales and children's stories, whose goal is to convey a practical life lesson. The disarmingly simple style, paired with the book's non-denominational spiritual lesson, explains its appeal to readers of all tastes and people of all spiritual inclinations.

Character List

Santiago

Santiago is the protagonist of the *The Alchemist*. Born in a small town in Andalusia, Santiago attends the seminary as a boy but longs to travel the world. He finally gets the courage to ask his father's permission to become a shepherd so that he can travel the fields of Andalusia. One day, he meets a mysterious man in the town of Tarifa, who sends him on a journey to the other side of Africa.

Santiago is a curious boy whose open mind makes him particularly suited to finding his Personal Legend. He also values his freedom very highly, which is why he became a shepherd and why he is reticent to get involved in things which threaten his freedom. In the end, he realizes that playing it safe is often more threatening to his freedom than taking a risk.

Melchizedek

Melchizedek is the king of Salem, a mysterious far-off land. Melchizedek appears to Santiago in the town square of Tarifa, where he tells Santiago about the Soul of the World and his Personal Legend for the first time. Melchizedek always appears to people who are trying to live their Personal Legend, even if they don't know it. While he appears at first to be dressed in common Arab dress, at one point he pulls aside his cloak to reveal a gold breastplate encrusted with precious stones. He also gives Santiago the magical stones Urim and Thummim.

The Englishman

Santiago meets the Englishman on the caravan to Al-Fayoum. The Englishman is trying to become a great alchemist and is traveling to Al-Fayoum to study with a famous alchemist who is rumored to be over 200 years old and to have the ability to turn any metal into gold. Santiago learns much about alchemy from the Englishman, who lends Santiago his books while they travel across the Sahara.

Fatima

A beautiful girl who lives at the Al-Fayoum oasis. Santiago falls in love with her at the well there. He and Fatima talk everyday for several weeks, and finally he asks her to marry him. Fatima, however, insists that he seek out his Personal Legend before they marry. This perplexes Santiago, but the Alchemist teaches him that true love never gets in the way of one's Personal Legend. If it does, then it is not true love.

The Alchemist

Very powerful alchemist who lives at the Al-Fayoum oasis in Egypt. Initially, Santiago hears about him through the Englishman, but eventually Santiago reveals himself to be the Alchemist's true disciple. The Alchemist dresses in all black and uses a falcon to hunt for game. The Alchemist is also in possession of the Elixir of Life and the Philosopher's Stone.

The Shopkeeper

Gives Santiago a job in Tangiers after he has been robbed. Santiago takes the job at the crystal shop and learns much about the shopkeeper's attitude toward life and the importance of dreaming. The shopkeeper, while generally afraid to take risks, is a very kind man and understands Santiago's quest - sometimes more than Santiago himself. This is the case when the shopkeeper tells Santiago that he will not return to Spain, since it it is not his fate.

Major Themes

Dreams (Sleeping)

It is a dream that first leads Santiago to pursue his destiny. It is also a dream (although someone else's dream) that sends him back.

Santiago dreams of a child showing him a treasure at the base of the Pyramids; when we first read of the dream, we are led to believe that Santiago has had it before. When he tells the gypsy of Tarifa and Melchizedek about this dream, they both implore him to follow it, because, they argue, dreams are the language in which the Universe speaks. At the end of the book, it is the dream of the robber–which was the exact inverse of Santiago's dream, showing the treasure at the abandoned church–that sends Santiago back to Spain and to the treasure. The theme of dreams is linked, then, with the theme of fate, since dreams are the way in which people come to know their destiny.

Love

When the story of *The Alchemist* begins, the reader finds Santiago looking forward to a rendezvous with a merchant's daughter he met the previous year. As soon as he is convinced to go in search of his treasure, however, Santiago forgets all about the girl. Then he meets Fatima at the Al-Fayoum oasis, and thinks about giving up his quest to be with her. The difference between the two cases is two-fold.

First, what Santiago felt for the merchant girl was not love. It was merely an attraction that had no spiritual element to it. For this reason it was very easy for Santiago to shrug her off and continue with his fate. In the case of Fatima, though, everything is different. The first time that Santiago and Fatima see one another, Santiago feels that the Soul of the World is speaking directly to him. Secondly, Fatima does not encourage Santiago to abandon his Personal Legend. It is for this reason that Fatima's love does not prevent him from pursuing his fate. Since Fatima is part of Santiago's fate, she does not stand in the way of his Personal Legend. This is the fundamental difference between true love and all other love and one of the main themes of *The Alchemist* - namely, that true love never gets in the way of living one's life to the fullest. If one has to choose between a Personal Legend and love then that love is not true love after all.

Fate

One of the fundamental themes of *The Alchemist* is that our paths are pre-ordained or *maktub*, in the words of the shopkeeper. The goal of life is to live in harmony with what is ordained for one, or one's Personal Legend; happiness depends upon this harmony. Ostensibly, we all once knew, as children, what our Personal Legends were. The main problem is that as humans and adults, we strive to make things more complex than they really are. In the text of *The Alchemist*, this problem is mirrored by the experience Santiago has with alchemy. While traveling through the desert with the Englishman, Santiago reads several books about the secrets of alchemy. The books claim that the original secret of alchemy could be written in a single sentence, but that mankind had made its explanations of that secret so convoluted that they could not be understood by anyone. Santiago rejects this and contends that he can learn everything he needs to know about alchemy through his day-to-day life. This conviction, that one's fate, or Personal Legend, is apparent in any aspect of one's normal life forms one of the most important themes of *The Alchemist*. When Melchizedek says, "When you want something, all the universe is conspiring to help you achieve it," (22) he means that since it is fate that puts a desire in Santiago's heart, fate won't stop him from achieving it. The problem is focusing one's energy on determining what it is that one *really* wants. Santiago does this during the last leg of his journey with the Alchemist, when he learns from the desert to look inside himself and silence his petty fears. By silencing these fears, he is able to finally see that he is one with the world around him and that his Personal Legend is a harmonious part of that world. This is evinced in a magical fashion when Santiago is able to communicate with the elements, in the climactic scene in which he turns himself into the wind.

Unity

The unity of all existence can be traced as a theme through two main aspects of the narrative. First, as Coelho describes it, the Soul of the World unites us all - people, plants, rocks and elements. Second, that there is no significant difference between the different religions of the world. In the narrative of *The Alchemist*, this unity of humans and the natural world is pointed out several times. One example is the Alchemist's assertion that even material elements have a Personal Legend. The reason that alchemists can turn any metal into gold is because it is the Personal Legend of that common metal to become gold. Alchemists help elements achieve their Personal Legends in much the same way as the Alchemist helps Santiago realize his own Legend. This unity with the natural world can also be seen when Santiago converses with the wind, the desert and, finally, the one hand which wrote everything. This, the reader is to understand, is God.

In a sense, the final realization of the book is that Santiago's soul is just a part of the Soul of the World, which is the same as God. This in turn translates in to a much more pragmatic ecumenicist theme in the book - that is to say, that throughout the narrative there is a minimization of the difference between Muslim and Christian, the two religious spheres in which the narrative takes place. The reader is led to understand that since God is one with all of creation, all religions are essentially saying the same thing. Thus, Santiago's initial thoughts about the strangeness of the "infidels," as he first refers to the residents of the city of Tangiers, are quite quickly swept away by his realization that the spiritual concerns of Muslims are very similar to his own. The shopkeeper's concerns about his dream of pilgrimage to Mecca can be identified with any dream that one is afraid of fulfilling.

Selfishness

The book opens with a prologue which retells the story of Narcissus, bringing the question of selfishness to the fore. In the traditional telling of the story of Narcissus, Narcissus drowns in a lake because he is so enamored with his own reflection that he falls in. In the prologue's unique retelling, it is revealed that while Narcissus was selfish, the lake in which Narcissus drowned was also selfish. After Narcissus' death, the lake misses him because it could contemplate itself in his eyes. This already tells the reader that the theme of selfishness will not be treated in a one-sided, moralizing manner.

Selfishness reappears in the form of the Personal Legend. The Personal Legend is something which a person truly desires with all of his/her heart. The novel suggests that the only thing that is important in life is to pursue this dream at whatever cost. Often this means avoiding things which are not conducive to achieving this dream. In the case of Santiago, this means leaving his familial home. It also means that any love which he experiences must not get in the way of his Personal Legend.

The novel states that, since the Personal Legend is placed in one's heart by Fate or the Soul of the World, pursuing the Personal Legend is not an option; it is instead one's duty. *The Alchemist* thus suggests that selfishness is not necessarily evil, but is to a degree the only way to live at peace with the universe and to be happy.

Dreams (Aspirations)

Dreams in the sense of "goals" or "aspirations" also constitute a major theme. Santiago's dream of the treasure provides him with a goal; Santiago resolves to find the treasure, and by his decision to pursue this goal he is able to realize his Personal Legend. Thus, Coelho plays with the dual (and of course linked) meanings of the word "dream", as both visions during slumber and far-reaching objectives. In this sense, the message of *The Alchemist* could be described as follows: everyone needs a dream. The vulnerable periods of Santiago's journey are when he has no clearly defined goal. This is true when he finishes working at the crystal shop, as well as when he contemplates staying at the oasis with Fatima. Both times he thinks about desisting, but winds up carrying on unswayed.

As a counterpoint, we can think of the shopkeeper, who is afraid to realize his dream of going to Mecca. He does not want to achieve his dream because he feels that it is the only thing keeping him looking forward to the future. Santiago tries to show him that if it is his destiny, he has no choice but to seek it out, or else he is not living. In this way, *The Alchemist* is not about *what* one should dream, but merely that one should dream.

Glossary of Terms

Alchemy

The occult science which claims to be able to turn any common metal into gold.

Bedouin

Nomadic tribes that live in the African desert.

Breastplate

Large metal plate worn on the chest as part of a suit of armor. It is used for self defense, but can also be decorative.

Caravan

A group which travels through the desert. Travelers band together for mutual protection.

Language of the Universe

Omens, coincidences and dreams are the means by which the universe seeks to communicate. By remaining open to these omens, Santiago is able to learn more about the world and about himself.

Levanter

The name of the wind that blows off of Africa into Spain. So called because it comes from "the Levant." It is related to the conquest of Spain by the Moors. Santiago thinks that it brings the scent of exotic women and adventure.

Maktub

An Arabic word meaning "written." The shopkeeper uses it to refer to those thing preordained, or written, by Allah.

Moor

Spanish and European name for the Arabs that ruled the Iberian peninsula for almost 500 years.

Personal Legend

A Personal Legend is a true desire, which comes from the Soul of the Universe. This is different from other selfish desires in that the universe conspires to help you realize your personal legend. The story of *The Alchemist* is the story of Santiago realizing his Personal Legend.

Sacristy

Room where the vestments of the church are kept.

Sahara

The desert that runs across the width of the African continent. Known for its size and its harshness.

Scarab

A type of desert beetle which was sacred to the Ancient Egyptians. They believed that it symbolized the Sun and spiritual rebirth.

Shear

To cut, specifically the wool from a sheep.

Simum

A wind which blows through the desert and destroys everything in its path. A very strong sandstorm.

Soul of the World

A term which comes up repeatedly in the text, the Soul of the World is sometimes equated with God. It is a spiritual force that binds all of us together and governs all things and that speaks with us in the language of signs or omens.

The Elixir of Life

The Elixir of Life is the liquid portion of the Master Work, the goal of all alchemists. The Elixir of Life heals diseases and grants long life when ingested. The Alchemist carries some in a flask through the desert.

The Master Work

The Master Work is a term which refers, in alchemy, to the Elixir of Life and the Philosopher's Stone as a whole. The Master Work is the goal of all alchemists; the Alchemist has achieved it, but the Englishman is still seeking it.

The Philosophers Stone

The Philosophers Stone is the solid portion of the Master Work. The Philosopher's Stone has the ability to turn any metal into gold, an ability which the Alchemist uses to generate gold at the Coptic monastery in Egypt before taking his leave of Santiago.

Umim and Thummim

Two stones given to Santiago by Melchizedek. Melchizedek instructs Santiago to use them when he cannot read the omens of the world. These stones are drawn from a bag, with one signifying no and the other one signifying yes.

Zeal

Extreme enthusiasm, can sometimes be used pejoratively in the case of calling one a "zealot."

Short Summary

The Alchemist tells the story of a young shepherd named Santiago who is able to find a treasure beyond his wildest dreams. Along the way, he learns to listen to his heart and, more importantly, realizes that his dreams, or his Personal Legend, are not just his but part of the Soul of the Universe.

Santiago is a humble shepherd whose desires are few–he wants to be free to roam with his sheep, to have some wine in his wineskin and a book in his bag. Fate intervenes, however, in the form of the recurring dream of a great treasure hidden thousands of miles away at the base of the Egyptian Pyramids. When Santiago meets Melchizedek, a strange wise man who claims he is a king from a far-off land, he decides to seek his treasure. The next day, Santiago sells his sheep and embarks to Africa to pursue his dream.

Upon arriving in Africa, though, it becomes apparent that things will not be as easy as he thought. The first day Santiago is in Tangiers, he is robbed and left completely alone, unable to speak a single word of Arabic. At first Santiago contemplates giving up and turning around. He remembers the words of the wise man, though, and decides to carry on–getting a job at a local crystal shop. After working at the crystal shop for a year, learning much about life and about his Personal Legend, Santiago earns enough money to buy a new flock of sheep and return home. At the last minute, though, Santiago decides to risk it all and join a caravan to Egypt.

Once in the caravan, Santiago meets an Englishman who has come all the way to Africa to seek a renowned alchemist. As they travel through the desert, the Englishman tells Santiago about the secrets of alchemy. Santiago finds the Englishman's ideas to be very similar to Melchizedek's. They both speak of a Soul of the World to which we are all connected and of the necessity of following our heart's true desires or our Personal Legend. Santiago, however, prefers to learn these secrets by observing the world, while the Englishman prefers to learn from complex books. While they travel, they begin to hear rumors of a coming tribal war.

When they finally arrive at the Al-Fayoum oasis–the home of the titular Alchemist–Santiago meets a beautiful girl named Fatima with whom he immediately falls in love. He discovers that love, like the Personal Legend, comes directly from the Soul of the World. While walking in the desert, Santiago has a vision of an upcoming battle. He rushes back to warn the elders at the oasis and, when his vision is confirmed, they offer him a position as a counselor. Santiago considers staying at the oasis with Fatima, but the Alchemist finds Santiago and tells him that he will lead Santiago to his treasure.

Once again on the move, the Alchemist teaches Santiago to listen to his heart. Hearts can be treacherous, but the best way to keep them from fooling you is to listen to them intently. Almost to the pyramids, Santiago and the Alchemist are taken prisoner by a warring tribe. The Alchemist tells the tribesmen that Santiago is a powerful magician who can turn himself into the wind. The tribesmen are impressed and will spare the lives of the men if Santiago can do it. The only problem is that Santiago has no idea what he is doing. After three days of meditating, Santiago uses his knowledge of the Soul of the World to ask the elements to help him. First he asks the desert, then he asks the wind, then he asks the sun and, finally, he asks the Soul of the World. Immediately, the wind whips up, and Santiago disappears and reappears on the other side of the camp.

The Alchemist takes his leave of Santiago, who continues on to the Pyramids. Once there, Santiago is attacked by robbers. Asked what he is doing there, Santiago replies that he had a dream of a treasure buried at the base of the Pyramids. One of the robbers laughs at him, and says that he has had the exact same dream, except that in his the treasure was buried in Spain. Santiago realizes that the treasure was back in Spain the entire time.

The story then jumps forward in time and finds Santiago digging a hole at the base of the tree where he had had his first dream. Sure enough, he finds a trunk full of gold—enough for him and Fatima to live happily for a long time.

Quotes and Analysis

"In order to arrive you must follow the signs. God inscribed on the world the path that each man must follow. It is just a matter of reading the inscription he wrote for you."

The Alchemist

The notion of a universal language spoken by all creation is an important one in *The Alchemist*. This language manifests itself in signs presented by nature. Coelho underscores his concept of an all-encompassing unity, tying language (commonly considered a peculiarly human faculty) to the rest of nature. The world is itself a text, full of meanings to be deciphered and taught.

"Everything on the face of the Earth is constantly being transformed because the Earth is alive and has a Soul."

The Alchemist

Everything on Earth is related. This is because everything, including inanimate objects, has a soul, and that soul is connected to the Soul of the World. Santiago's ability to communicate with the forces of nature (such as the Wind and the Desert) is itself both an act of communication across perceived divides and an act of transformation. That which is not living cannot communicate; the Earth engages in conversation and is thus a living being - just like Santiago.

"You don't have to understand the desert: all you have to do is contemplate a simple grain of sand, and you will see in it all the marvels of creation."

The Alchemist

The alchemist is urging simplicity. In Coelho's book, alchemy itself has become impossibly convoluted, when once upon a time the simplest of formulas could turn a common stone to gold. Now, the alchemist (and, by extension one could argue, Coelho) considers a vast desert - from a visual standpoint, the simplest of terrains - and argues to Santiago that all beauty, all marvel, all complexity can be found within a given speck of that terrain.

"A blessing rejected becomes a curse."

The Alchemist

This quote recalls the Santiago's temporary desire to delay the pursuit of the treasure in order to stay with Fatima. While this seems like a good idea at the time, the alchemist, who utters these words, knows that the decision will only lead to resentment in the future.

"Anyone who interferes in the destiny of others will never discover his own."

Along Santiago's journey, he begins to realize that everyone must pursue his/her Personal Legend in his/her own distinct way. This lesson is illustrated by the Englishman, who is pursuing his Personal Legend through complicated books of alchemy. Santiago realizes that though this may not be his path or the path he would choose, it is nonetheless a legitimate path.

"God exists wherever He is allowed to enter."

The Alchemist

The secrets of the universe were once known to everyone. The reason they are unknown now is not because they are complicated, but rather because we, as humans, complicated them. Therefore, as this quote suggests, finding God or happiness is not always a matter of seeking Him out, but rather of listening to the language of the World.

"Love never keeps a man from pursuing his personal legend. If he abandons that pursuit, it's because it wasn't true love."

The Alchemist

The alchemist utters these words to Santiago in reference to the romance with Fatima. This quote thus signals a major turning point in the novel, the moment at which Santiago must choose between the short-term pleasures of his romance and his stay in the oasis and the lingering quest to achieve his Personal Legend. What the alchemist suggests is that true love comes with the Personal Legend as well; true love will never stand in the way. Fatima has already echoed this viewpoint in her urging Santiago to continue his quest. Coelho thus posits a definition of love as inextricably linked to (and perhaps subservient to) a person's individual goals in life and one's realization of the self.

Quotes and Analysis

Summary and Analysis of the Prologue

Summary

The Alchemist, a character who will not be introduced until much later in the narrative, finds a book that retells the myth of Narcissus. The myth of Narcissus traditionally tells how a youth, whose name was Narcissus, loved his own image so much that he spent days looking at his own reflection in a lake. One day, he was so infatuated with himself that he lost his concentration, slipped and drowned in the lake. A flower grew by where he fell and this plant came to be called the narcissus.

The author of the book the Alchemist finds is different, though. It continues by telling how the goddess of the forest went to the lake after Narcissus had died and found it converted into a lake of tears; the lake was *weeping* for Narcissus. The lake missed Narcissus because, in the reflection of his eyes, the lake could contemplate itself. This version of the myth makes the Alchemist very happy.

Analysis

This prologue introduces several elements which will come into play later in the narrative. First, the reader can see the attribution of human traits to inanimate objects - in this case, the lake that cries. This both sets the magical tone of the narrative and highlights the interrelation of all things, animate and inanimate, that forms one of the main themes of the book. Second, the story of the Narcissus highlights the question of selfishness, a question which is at the center of *The Alchemist*. Is it possible to pursue one's own personal desires while living a good life? In the case of Santiago, the answer is a resounding yes - making the image of Narcissus (who become a flower through his selfishness) especially apt.

Summary and Analysis of Part I.I

Summary

The story opens with the main character, the shepherd Santiago, arriving at an abandoned church with a sycamore growing in it in the Spanish region of Andalusia. He decides to stay the night at the church and corrals his herd into the church grounds. He falls asleep using the book that he keeps with him at all times as his pillow. During the night, he has a dream that he has had several times before, a dream he has never been able to fully understand. While waking his herd, he realizes that he is very close to the animals; they operate on the same schedule and he calls them all by name, convinced that they understand his conversation with them. They are very simple creatures, though, wanting only food and water. Recently all of this thoughts and conversations with the sheep have been about a girl he met a year ago, at the town that is his next destination. She is the daughter of a merchant and he has been thinking about her ever since he left.

Remembering their first meeting, Santiago reminisces about how he went to the shop of the girl's father to sell him some wool. While waiting for the shopkeeper to see him, the boy sat down to read a book. A voice from behind him said, "I didn't know shepherds knew how to read." The voice was that of the shopkeeper's daughter, a beautiful Andalusian girl whose features recalled the Moorish influence of the region. The girl and Santiago waited for two hours, during which time they told each other about their experiences, she in the town and he in the fields. The girl asked him why he was a shepherd if he had been to school and knew how to read. Santiago changed the subject and continued the conversation. He felt something which he had never felt before: the desire to stay in one place forever. Unfortunately, at that moment, the shopkeeper appeared, bought four sheep worth of wool and told the boy to come back in a year.

Leaving the church in the morning, Santiago is both excited and apprehensive about seeing the girl. She could have forgotten him. As they set out, he begins to think about the lives of the sheep, and how sheep don't make any decisions. They want only food and water and rely on Santiago for that. Surprised at his feelings of mild resentment toward the animals, Santiago decides his recurring dream has made him uneasy. When he gets to the town, he resolves, he will tell the girl why he knows how to read, how he went to seminary and was originally set to be a priest, and one day got the courage to tell his family that he would rather travel the world as a shepherd. As we learn from Santiago's memories, his father at first tried to convince him to stay, pointing out that plenty of travelers had passed through their lands and said that they would like to live there. In the end, however, he capitulated and gave Santiago his blessing and three old gold coins to buy his flock. Santiago could thus see that his father himself had once had dreams of traveling the world.

Santiago's lifestyle as a shepherd has provided him with a lot of freedom. All he has to do is allow his sheep to lead the way for a while and he will always find a new path. The difference between him and the sheep, though, is that the sheep never know they are on a new path. Once again, all they think about is food and water. Santiago realizes that dreaming about what you don't have is what makes life interesting.

Analysis

Part I of the novel, which ends with Santiago accepting a job at the crystal shop, includes the main character's introduction, acceptance of challenge and initial setback. The reader is also introduced, in an unexplained form, to several of the main terms that reappear and are explained throughout the story, among them "Personal Legend" and "Soul of the World." This section also introduces several of the main themes of the narrative: love, in the false-love of Santiago for the merchant's daughter; dreams, in the form of Santiago's dream of the treasure; fate, in the form of Melchizedek's intervention in Santiago's life.

The narrative arc of *The Alchemist* follows a relatively common formula. The hero leaves home to pursue a quest, is tested three times, and, upon succeeding, returns home as a victor. What makes *The Alchemist* stand apart, though, is that there are essentially two parallel quests going on in the narrative. The first is a rather familiar search for treasure. This quest, though, is merely the metaphorical double to Santiago's other journey, which is to discover his own Personal Legend. What is particularly interesting about this section is the way that (similarly to this narrative dichotomy) it straddles the great geographic division that forms the main dialectic of the physical story - namely, that between Spain and Africa. While the end of this section could have very easily come when Santiago leaves Andalusia for Africa, it instead concludes when Santiago seems to have resigned himself to merely make enough money to return to Spain. This division suggests that the main drama in the narrative is not a physical adventure–characterized by exotic lands, physical challenges or vicious enemies–but rather an interior drama (of Santiago overcoming his own fears and harnessing the willpower to achieve his Personal Legend).

The book Santiago carries with him at all times has several symbolic resonances. It distinguishes him from being a common shepherd. The merchant girl knows that he is extraordinary because he can read. The book is a source of knowledge and freedom, allowing Santiago a different, broader outlook on the world. Books also, however, propagate certain misleading ideas, as argued by Melchizedek when he claims that Santiago's book endorses the world's greatest lie. Later, the Englishman will be blocked from realizing the truths of alchemy because he is too tied to his complicated books. Fate is often described metaphorically as a book that was written by one hand. The "book of fate" would thus be the only book capable of telling the whole truth.

This section also introduces the Moors, who will recur throughout the novel. The merchant girl, of whom Santiago dreams, is remarkable for her "moorish" features. This foreshadows both Santiago's love for Fatima and the journey he will undertake to Africa, from whence the Moors came.

Summary and Analysis of Part I.II

Summary

Once Santiago gets to Tarifa, his last stop before the city where the shopkeeper's daughter lives, he goes to see an old gypsy woman who interprets dreams, with the hope that she will help him understand his own recurring dream. When reliving the dream, just as the child is about to show Santiago the location of the treasure, Santiago wakes up. The Gypsy woman tells him that this treasure is real and that he must go to the Pyramids, an interpretation for which she charges him one-tenth of this future treasure.

Upon leaving the Gypsy's house, Santiago sits in the Plaza to read a book, where he meets an old man who is eager to strike up a conversation. It turns out that the old man not only knows how to read but has read the book that Santiago is struggling through. The man reveals himself to be Melchizedek, the King of Salem, and he introduces Santiago to what he calls "the world's greatest lie." The World's Greatest Lie states that fate prevents one from achieving his/her Personal Legend. Everyone has a Personal Legend, or something which he/she has wanted to achieve his/her entire life. Personal Legends come from the Soul of the World and this Soul of the World conspires to help everyone achieve them. Unfortunately, fear and routine get in the way. Melchizedek explains to Santiago that he appears to those who truly want to realize their Personal Legends: sometimes he appears as a stone, sometime he appears as a king. Melchizedek seems to be able to read Santiago's mind and promises to tell him about the treasure in his dream if he gives him one-tenth of his sheep.

After much deliberation, Santiago decides that his sheep, the merchant's daughter and the fields of Andalusia were just steps on his way to his Personal Legend, and so he decides to sell his flock and gives six to Melchizedek right away. Melchizedek takes the sheep and advises Santiago to always follow the omens, for they are the language of the universe. Melchizedek also gives Santiago two stones, a black stone called Urim (meaning "yes") and a white stone called Thummim (meaning "no"). Santiago is to consult these if he cannot understand the omens. Santiago buys a ticket from Tarifa to Africa and sets sail to find his treasure and his Personal Legend.

Upon arriving in Tangiers, Santiago realizes that his journey will be a lot more difficult than he expected. The problem? He doesn't speak Arabic. Sitting in a bar alone, he is approached by a young man who speaks Spanish and offers to help him get to the Pyramids. The young man takes Santiago to buy a camel and manages to escape with all of Santiago's money in the confusion of the marketplace. Santiago weeps with despair, but he asks the stones Urimm and Thummim if the Melchizedek's blessing is still with him. They answer 'Yes', and Santiago resolves to continue his journey.

Wandering the streets of Tangiers, Santiago comes across a crystal shop that has fallen on hard times. After Santiago cleans the pieces in the front window, the owner offers him a job. The owner tells Santiago that he will pay Santiago enough to save up for a new flock of sheep and a passage back to Andalusia. Santiago agrees and takes the job.

Analysis

This part of *The Alchemist* finds Santiago changing the course of his life by deciding to give up his profession - a sort of safe haven for him - and to pursue his dream. This is the first of many episodes in the book wherein the desire to play it safe and to stick with what one knows almost holds Santiago back. Ironically, Santiago took a risk in becoming a shepherd in the first place. He wanted the freedom to roam the countryside and to get to know different regions, different towns. But after meeting Melchizedek, Santiago realizes that those things which seemed to offer him freedom have come to imprison him.

Also introduced in this section is the theme of dreams as meaningful and portentous. We have heard f Santiago's dream before, but only now do we hear a possible interpretation of it; only now does it become a call for action. The Gypsy claims that dreams are a language used by the Soul of the World to communicate with people. They are part of the fabric of a universal language that binds beings together.

Through this description of dreams, and the events that unfold in the narrative, Coelho's magical, fairy-tale style takes shape and comes to the fore. Melchizedek is himself a fantastical character, who knows a positively *super*natural amount of things about Santiago's personal life, has magical stones to offer, and claims to be able to turn himself into different things. In this way, *The Alchemist* shows a certain amount of affinity with magical realism - a genre of literature wherein fantastic things happen but the characters react to them in psychologically realistic ways. This magical tone is one of the dominant stylistic characteristics of the novel.

When Santiago first travels to Africa, the reader sees his vaguely skeptical attitude toward the Muslims he meets. While in the bar, he hears the call to prayer and watches the Muslims prostrate themselves on the ground. He remarks that their actions are those of infidels. He also calls to mind St. Matamoros (literally 'kills moors') who is depicted on a mighty steed slaying the infidels at his feet. As the novel continues, these views will change, and the image of St. Matamoros will later recur in an altogether different circumstance.

Summary and Analysis of Part II.I

Summary

After working at the crystal shop for a month, Santiago suggests that the shop owner build a display case for the crystal to attract new customers. The owner seems resistant to change, as if he is afraid of success. The owner then tells Santiago that, although he has always dreamed of making the pilgrimage to Mecca, he knows he will never do it. He tells Santiago that he is afraid that, once he achieves his dream, he will have no need to go on living. Santiago ends up convincing him on certain issues, and within the year Santiago spends working at the shop, the owner makes several changes that improve business. At the end of the year Santiago resolves to take the money he has saved, buy a flock of sheep and return to Spain. As he takes his leave, he asks the shopkeeper for his blessing; the shopkeeper gives it, but tells Santiago that he knows he will not return to Spain. The shopkeeper reiterates that he himself will likewise never go to Mecca. He claims that this is *maktub* - or written by God. Santiago realizes that while he is far from home, he is actually closer than ever to the Pyramids and the treasure. He resolves to take a chance and join a caravan across the desert in search of his treasure.

When Santiago goes to the stable to take the caravan, he meets an Englishman, who is in search of a famous alchemist living in Al-Fayoum oasis. The Englishman is obsessed with finding the common language of all the world and has spent the majority of his inheritance traveling and studying science, religion, and finally, alchemy.

While Santiago and the Englishman are waiting for the caravan to leave, Santiago takes out Urim and Thummim and the Englishman immediately recognizes them. He carries the same two stones in his own pocket. He goes on to tell Santiago that it is not accidental that the two of them met on the caravan. Coincidences and omens are the universal language that the whole world can understand. It is the task of alchemy to decipher this language. Santiago realizes that the series of events which led him to this point - meeting Melchizedek getting robbed and happening upon the shopkeeper and the crystal shop - where not accidental or random at all but were signs that he is nearing his Personal Legend.

The caravan begins to move across the desert, and Santiago learns many things from the English alchemist and the guides of the caravan. The desert is enormous and dangerous, and the guides teach Santiago about listening to its language of omens. The Englishman refers to the Soul of the Word and describes it as the principle that governs all things. When we have an intuition or truly want something, we are immersed in the Soul of the World. This is not a strictly human gift, though; everything on the face of the earth has a soul and a Personal Legend. Santiago is interested and asks to borrow the Englishman's books about alchemy.

Reading the Englishman's books, Santiago learns more about alchemy. He finds out that the goal of alchemy is the Master Work. The Master Work is part liquid and part solid; the liquid is called the Elixir of Life and the solid is called the Philosopher's Stone. The Englishman's books tell the stories of all the famous alchemists who dedicated their lives to realizing their Personal Legends. As he reads on, Santiago realizes that he and the English alchemist are pursuing the same thing, but Santiago prefers to read the omens of the world in his everyday life instead of in old musty books.

While the caravan moves across the desert, there is a war brewing amongst the tribes of the region. It is becoming more and more dangerous by the day, but the caravan has no choice but to carry on and hope for the best. From the stoic guides of the caravan, Santiago learns the value of concentrating on the present.

Analysis

Part II of *The Alchemist* shows Santiago encountering two more setbacks before he can reach his destination. Part of the artistry of Coelho's narrative lies in the way Santiago's setbacks, or complications, become progressively more and more complicated. While the first setback - getting robbed in Tangiers - is admittedly serious, it is also relatively prosaic. Looking ahead, the second setback, Santiago's love for Fatima, is more complicated because love is not usually presented as a setback. Santiago, however, contemplates suspending his quest, something not even being robbed in a foreign land could do, to stay with Fatima. The reader sees, once again, Santiago pondering his options and relying, once again, on outside intervention to make his decision. Even though Fatima tells Santiago that she wants him to continue, he is still undecided. At this point, fate intervenes both in the form of the omen in the desert and the alchemist telling Santiago his future of resentment and regret if he doesn't pursue his dream. As a result, once again, Santiago continues.

The final complication, Santiago's feat of turning himself into the wind, is different in a few ways. First of all, it is by far the most profound. Whereas the first two were essentially physical and personal setbacks, the last one is spiritual in nature. Santiago comes to realize that he and God are one soul and that his soul is a small part of the greater Soul of the World. Secondly, the last complication is different in that Santiago overcomes it entirely by himself. There is no intervention on the part of the Alchemist or anyone else. This is in keeping with the dual-narrative modality at play in *The Alchemist* - a physical narrative and arc paralleled by a spiritual equivalent. The scene wherein Santiago turns himself into the wind is the climax of the spiritual journey, just as the discovery of the treasure is the climax of the physical journey.

By working at the crystal shop, Santiago learns many lessons. One of the most important is that it does not take an exterior force to prevent one from realizing one's dreams. The shopkeeper is actively trying to avoid achieving his dream, because he believes that if he achieves it he will have nothing to aspire to. It is with this in mind that Santiago decides to continue on his own quest.

The theme of fate is touched upon again in the meeting of the Englishman and Santiago. In many ways, these two form two sides of the same character - the seeker of knowledge. In many ways, they are both seeking a treasure: the Englishman wants to learn how to turn lead into gold and Santiago is seeking a buried treasure. Both of them, however, realize that there is much more at stake than just material wealth. They are different in that the Englishman insists on learning everything from books. These books form the basis of all of his knowledge, so much so that the real world is secondary. Santiago, on the other hand, is constantly learning by observing the world, the desert, the omens of life. The characters are, however, intimately joined by fate.

Summary and Analysis of Part II.II

Summary

Finally the caravan reaches the oasis, where the alchemist awaits its arrival. (He has known from reading the various omens of the desert that there is someone in the caravan who is seeking him out.) It makes the old alchemist happy to see the travelers arrive, to see them so elated at the sight of palm trees after so much sand.

The war amongst the tribes makes the desert too dangerous to pass, so the caravan must stay at the oasis indefinitely. This gives the Englishman time to seek out the alchemist. With Santiago helping him, the Englishman begins to question people about the alchemist's whereabouts. In the process of asking, Santiago meets a beautiful girl at the well and falls immediately in love. He realizes that when you are in love you hear the language of the Soul of the World perfectly. Her name is Fatima and he begins to meet her at the well every day and tell her his story and of all the things that he has learned. Finally, he tells Fatima he wants to marry her. He even thinks about giving up his quest to the Pyramids to be with her. Fatima, however, tells Santiago that she understands his need to go find the treasure, and that she in fact wants him to realize his goal. The women of the desert, she explains, are proud of their men's freedom. This confuses Santiago, who is unable to separate love and possession. While thinking about this alone on the outskirts of the oasis, Santiago has a vision of an invading army. After consulting one of the guides of the caravan, Santiago resolves to tell the chiefs of the oasis what the omens of the desert have shown him.

Santiago tells the chiefs and, after some deliberation, they decide to ready themselves for war - even though this is against the tradition of the oasis, which is usually considered neutral ground. The chiefs make a stipulation: if the enemy arrives, the chief will give Santiago a piece of gold for every 10 enemies slain; if Santiago's vision is wrong, he will be killed. Walking home from his meeting with the chiefs Santiago is pensive but sure that he has made the right decision. Suddenly, he is assailed by a man with a falcon on his shoulder, dressed all in black, riding a white horse. The man holds a sword to Santiago's head and demands to know how he knew of the coming of the army. Santiago, frightened, explains to the man about the omens of the desert and his Personal Legend, concluding that he had no choice. The man understands completely, to Santiago's surprise, and takes his leave, telling Santiago to come see him if he survives the coming days. As the horseman rides away, Santiago realizes that he has just met the alchemist.

The next day, 500 armed tribesmen enter the oasis as Santiago has predicted. The men of the oasis, duly warned, kill all of the intruders and the chieftain of the oasis awards Santiago 50 pieces of gold and asks him to become the oasis's counselor.

That night, Santiago seeks out the alchemist and finds his tent. The alchemist tells Santiago to prove that he can read the language of omens by finding life in the desert. Santiago trusts his horse to guide him to life, and they find a snake which the alchemist neutralizes with a spell. Satisfied, the alchemist offers to lead Santiago across the desert to the treasure. Santiago is conflicted because he wants to stay at the oasis with Fatima. The alchemist responds that "love never keeps a man from pursuing his personal legend. If he abandons that pursuit, it's because it wasn't true love...the love speaks the Language of the World." (120) Santiago decides to leave the next day with the alchemist.

Analysis

Over the course of this section, the alchemist implicitly chooses Santiago as his disciple over the Englishman. This is counterintuitive, considering that the Englishman is much more educated in the secrets of alchemy than Santiago. The alchemist, though, shows that the intuitive method of Santiago is preferable to the intellectual pursuit of the Englishman. Santiago has been trying to learn about the universe by diving into it, experiencing it, seeing, hearing, and tasting it - not just reading about it.

This section also showcases a substantial increase in Santiago's powers. He is now able to use his skills of divination to protect those that he cares about. He is tempted, however, to use these powers, acquired in order to pursue his Personal Legend, for short-term gain. In this way, the attraction of the position as a counselor of the oasis is an ethical dilemma. Santiago would be truly squandering his abilities if he were to use them for something as short-sighted as such a position. It can also be asked whether he would even retain said powers if he stayed at the oasis, since he would have given up on the sincere commitment which allowed him to achieve such powers in the first place.

Love comes to the fore in this part of the narrative, but it is complicated by the book's philosophy. Fatima, Santiago's love interest, tells him that she would rather him achieve his Personal Legend than stay by her side. Her reasoning is that she loves Santiago and therefore must love his dreams as well. The alchemist, who encourages Santiago to pursue his Personal Legend, has a slightly different logic. He claims that, although Santiago will be extremely happy for a while, he will come to resent Fatima for preventing him from achieving his dreams. It is better to pursue those dreams than to allow them to fester. The other side of this logic is that the alchemist claims that there can be no conflict between true love and one's Personal Legend. This is because true love is defined as that love which does get in the way of the Personal Legend. In this way, the novel sets up the Personal Legend as the central organizing principle of a spiritually fulfilled life. Once the Personal Legend is identified and committed to, all other things will become clear.

Summary and Analysis of Part II.III

Summary

After reaffirming his love to Fatima, Santiago sets across the desert with the alchemist. They travel in silence, eating the game that the alchemist's falcon brings them. Santiago grows restless, is hungry for more of the alchemist's secrets. The alchemist explains that Santiago has learned much, but the one thing that he has left to learn cannot be taught. He must learn it for himself. In the beginning, the alchemist explains, the secrets of the universe were known to all, but men have been complicating things because they seek the treasure of their Personal Legends, but do not with to *live* their Personal Legends. The alchemist advises Santiago to listen to his heart.

The two travel cautiously now, because they are nearing the area with the most warring tribes. Santiago listens to his heart and finds it agitated. It begins to tell him stories about the Soul of the World - about others who have failed to find their fortune. It is scared and wants to go back to Fatima. Santiago tells the alchemist that his heart is treasonous, that it does not want him to continue. "Treason is a blow that comes unexpectedly," comes the reply. "If you know your heart well, it will never be able to do that to you." (129)

As they travel, Santiago listens to his heart and eventually comes to be at peace with it. As the journey nears its end, Santiago tells the alchemist that he wants to know some secrets of alchemy. The alchemist tells Santiago that he already knows many important secrets; he knows that one must listen to the Soul of the World to find one's treasure. Every thing on earth, even minerals, has a Personal Legend. This is why alchemists can change any metal into gold: they are simply helping the metal achieve its Personal Legend.

The war finally catches up with the travelers and they are taken captive by a warring tribe. The tribesmen take them for spies and threaten to kill them. To save his and Santiago's lives, the alchemist gives the tribesmen all of Santiago's money and tells the tribesman that Santiago is a powerful wizard who can turn himself into the wind and destroy them. The tribesman don't believe him, but give Santiago three days to prove himself.

Santiago panics because he has no idea how to turn himself into the wind. The alchemist seems unconcerned. For three days, Santiago goes up on a cliff and contemplates the desert, listening to his heart. Finally, on the third day, he goes to the very top of the cliff and uses his heart to talk to the Desert - since they both speak the Language of the World. He asks the Desert to help him turn himself into the Wind, because he is love with a girl and wants desperately to go back to her, but the Desert does not know how. Next he asks the Wind, but the Wind does not know what love is. Finally he asks the Sun, who knows what love is, but cannot help Santiago. The

Sun suggests that Santiago ask the Hand that wrote all. Santiago then starts to pray - but that prayer emerges as not a request but an acknowledgement, as if culled from some deeper knowledge, that his heart and the Soul of the World are the same thing. Once Santiago comes to this realization, the wind begins to furiously blow and the tribesman find that Santiago has disappeared. He reappears on the other side of the camp. The tribal chiefs are so impressed that they let the travelers go and give them a guide so that they can reach their destination safely.

The next day, the alchemist and Santiago arrive at a coptic monastery. The alchemist uses his piece of the Philosopher's Stone to turn lead into a quantity of gold and gives some to Santiago and some to a monk. (He also gives an extra piece for the monk to hold onto for Santiago in case something should happen.) The alchemist takes his leave of Santiago, who travels farther and finally comes to the Pyramids. There he is overwhelmed with joy; he realizes all at once that he can turn back now, that the real treasure is not gold or jewels but the wisdom he has gained and his love for Fatima.

The alchemist told him, however, to listen to his heart. His heart tells him to start digging in the spot where he sees a scarab beetle. As he starts digging, a group of men approach him and beat him savagely, taking all of his money. When Santiago tries to explain what he is doing, one of the men tells him that he is a fool. He goes on to explain to Santiago that he had a recurring dream, too, depicting the same situation - but in Spain instead. He, however, was not stupid enough to go chasing after it, he remarks. After the robbers leave, Santiago gets up, elated. He now knows where his treasure lies.

Analysis

Traveling with the alchemist, Santiago learns many things that were merely hinted when he was traveling alone. It is with the alchemist that he finally realizes that his heart and soul are just little pieces of the Soul of the World. This is in keeping with the pantheism stressed throughout the whole of the book: God is one big soul, the Soul of the World. Because of this, all religions that recognize this fact are one and the same. This is the reasoning behind the ecumenicist thematic of the novel.

This section also contains the climax of the narrative, wherein the magical undercurrent of the novel comes to the fore. In this climax, Santiago talks to the elements: the Desert, the Wind, the Sun and finally the Soul of the World. A few aspects of this scene should be highlighted. First of all, we see that Santiago's communication with these inanimate forces is the realization of the alchemist's assertion that all things, even rocks and animals, have souls. What this essentially does is deny the dualism that we normally assume in our day to day lives: there is no real difference between things and beings. We are all beings with souls, some of whose characteristics are different than others.

Second, it is important to note that while Santiago talks to the Wind, the Desert and the Sun using words, when it comes time to communicate with the Soul of the World he cannot speak. This not to say, however, that he cannot *communicate*; what it means is that words are not sufficient. Communicating with the Soul of the Word ends up being a matter of opening his heart. This portrayal of language as lacking or insufficient is coherent with other parts of the novel wherein humanity is described as essentially fallen. The problem is not that the secrets of life are complicated, but that mankind has complicated these secrets through the use of language. The final step of Santiago's spiritual journey is therefore not accomplished through speaking, but through listening.

The twist at the story's end - that the treasure was always near Santiago after all - reinforces the teachings of the alchemist. Just as the alchemist insists that the secrets he holds are in fact simple and easy to understand, so too was the treasure always at home. Thus, the secrets to living a happier, more fulfilled life are not far away or exotic: they are quite often right in front of us, right under our noses. The rub is that often we must travel far and wide in order to realize this.

Summary and Analysis of Epilogue

Summary

Santiago arrives at the abandoned church as night falls and looks at the stars. He remembers when he and the alchemist looked at the stars while traveling in the desert and thinks about how far he has come both physically and spiritually. The next morning he begins digging, and within half an hour his shovel hits something hard. Within the next hour he has unearthed a huge chest full of gold and jewels. He remembers that he must go back to Tarifa to give the gypsy her share. When he is ready to leave he smells the wind blowing off the desert - bringing with it the kisses of Fatima.

Analysis

It is at this point in the narrative that the two parallel quests of Santiago come together. The fact that the physical treasure that Santiago sought was always close to home drives home the message that a spiritual journey is not about becoming someone else, but rather about finding oneself.

At the end of the narrative, Santiago returns to Fatima. This confirms what the Alchemist said about love: Santiago is able in the end to achieve both his Personal Legend and find his true love.

Suggested Essay Questions

1. **The prologue of *The Alchemist* includes a unique retelling of the myth of Narcissus. The traditional understanding of this myth is that it is a warning against self-love. What is the relationship of the prologue to the rest of the story?**

The main difference between the retelling of the Narcissus myth in the prologue of *The Alchemist* and the traditional telling is that, in the version in the prologue, the lake in which Narcissus drowns also misses Narcissus because it could regard itself in his eyes. Thus, the lake is itself selfish. In many ways, *The Alchemist* is all about selfishness. While society tends to regard the single-minded pursuit of one's dreams as selfish, the story proposes that this single-minded pursuit is not at odds with being a moral, happy person. Central to the story of *The Alchemist* is the idea that one's Personal Legend, or true desire, is not at odds with the organization of the universe. In fact, the opposite is true. Discovering one's Personal Legend is the only way to understand the greater secrets of the Soul of the World. This reversal of traditional views on selfishness is foreshadowed by the unique retelling of the Narcissus story.

2. **What is the significance of the fact that Santiago hails from the southern part of Spain? Do you think that the cultural history of this region affects the overall meaning of the book?**

One of the main themes of the book is the unity of all religions. The reader sees an equivalence between the beliefs of a Christian such as Santiago and a Muslim such as the shopkeeper. For this reason, the geography of southern Spain is very important, since it is both spatially and cultural linked to North Africa. This is also highlighted by the repeated references to "the invaders" - a reference to the Moorish domination of the Iberian peninsula. Santiago sees these figures as predominantly negative in the beginning of the story, but modifies his views toward the end. The location of the story allows for a sub-theme of tolerance and understanding.

3. **Fatima, Santiago's love interest, defines herself by her resignation to and support of Santiago's quest. What do you think the narrative is trying to say about the role of women or the role of love in general?**

Pursuing one's love interests as well as one's personal desires can often present a conflict. In *The Alchemist*, though, this conflict is alleviated by the fact that the two things need not be mutually exclusive. The primary purpose of one's life is one's Personal Legend. Once one identifies that, identifying true love is a relatively simple matter. True love is that love which does not get in the way of pursuing the Personal Legend. We must conclude, then, that love, although a powerful force in *The Alchemist*, is not primary. It is secondary to the Personal Legend. In the case of Fatima, she recognizes that Santiago must complete his mission or else he will not be living up to his potential. While this seems to relegate her to a supporting role, it is suggested that this is what she truly wants, and what is accepted by her community. Thus, in a way, she is also fulfilled.

4. **While Santiago's quest yields significant spiritual insights, its original motive is monetary gain. What is the narrative of *The Alchemist* trying to say about the relationship between material wealth and spirituality?**

The Alchemist suggests that the line between spiritual treasure and material treasure is not that fixed. While the relationship between the gold that Santiago finds and the spiritual discoveries he makes is largely metaphorical, the reader does see that the most important thing is not what you want, but just that you want that thing with all of your heart. In Santiago's case, that happens to be treasure. In the scheme of *The Alchemist* one can have both material and spiritual wealth.

5. *The Alchemist* **is clearly a novel about spiritual growth. Do you think that its message is at odds with organized religion?**

The novel espouses a kind of ecumenicist religion, wherein all religions are–at their core–one. The central ideas which bind these religions, Christianity and Islam in the case of the book, are a monotheistic God and the fact that that God has a certain fate determined for each person. The novel is also pantheist, in that each person's personal soul is part of the Soul of the World (a term which is interchangeable with God in this sense). God is not separate from us, but is rather the conjoined souls of all existence. The novel does not expressly go against organized religions in this sense, but it does show a lack of emphasis on certain elements of organized religion (such as ritual, hierarchy, etc.).

6. **Tradition plays a major role in Santiago's personal life and in the life of the people he meets in his travels. Describe the different viewpoints that the novel presents on tradition.**

There are two very different views of tradition put forth in *The Alchemist*. The novel begins with Santiago leaving his traditional home and the role that his family has chosen for him–the priesthood–in order to pursue his treasure. This seems to suggest that one's own Personal Legend is more important than tradition. On the other hand, the tribes in the desert repeatedly fall back on what they simply refer to as "The Tradition." This is a body of knowledge which tells them when to go to war, what visions to trust, etc. Thus we see here a culture that values tradition highly.

7. **When Santiago is lost and alone in Tangiers, the owner of the crystal shop offers him a position at his shop. What does Santiago learn from his time at the crystal shop?**

The owner of the crystal shop teaches Santiago that one of the principle things which endangers the pursuit of a dream is one's own fear of achieving it. The crystal shop owner wants to go to Mecca, but also fears that if he does so he might lose his reason for living. Up until that point, Santiago has only been acquainted with exterior interference with achieving one's dreams, such as being robbed.

8. **Although Melchizedek plays a major role in Santiago's decision to continue in search of his treasure, he only appears once in the book. Does he have any connection with the other characters that appear in the book?**

While Melchizedek only appears once in *The Alchemist* he does prefigure some of the other characters in the story. He explicitly tells Santiago that he sometimes appears as other things besides the King of Salem. For example, he tells Santiago a story wherein he appears as a stone. Santiago also recognizes elements of Melchizedek's personality and philosophy in other characters, such as the shopkeeper and the Alchemist.

9. **How do you think the style of *The Alchemist* affects its meaning?**

The novel is written in a very plain style, using short declarative sentences and few modifiers such as adjectives and adverbs. The book also makes wide use capitalized terminology and magical situations such as visions and communication with the Wind, Desert, etc. These combined factors make the didactic thrust of the story apparent. By simplifying the psychology of the characters and featuring characters with no names (the Englishman, the Alchemist, etc.), the story takes on a more universal appeal.

10. **Does the fact that Paulo Coelho is Brazilian affect the meaning of the novel in any way?**

The Andalusia and Africa of Santiago have very little to do with historical reality. While this can be dismissed as a lack of realism on Coelho's part, it might also be due to the fact that, since Coelho is not Spanish, he is able to approach the subject matter without being encumbered by material reality. As an outsider, Coelho is able to write not about what life in Spain and Africa is like, but what it could be like.

Paulo Coelho's Reception in Brazil

In many ways, Paulo Coelho's career has faced the same difficulties as other wildly successful writers. He is simultaneously adored by millions of fans around the world and completely reviled by the literati of every country his books have conquered. This could not be more true than in Brazil, a country whose literary community feels maligned for lack of attention, and a country whose literary tradition only receives attention for its most commercial, light productions. The world, especially the English-speaking world, does not regularly consider Brazil among the great literary traditions, and Brazil was somehow excised from the general fervor surrounding Latin American fiction in the 60s with the rise or Garcia-Marquez, Vargas Llosa, etc. Essentially, Brazil's two best (internationally) known authors have been Jorge Amado and Paulo Coelho. While the substance of the accusation is different in each cases, both of these writers have been accused of being simplistic and sub-literary. Jorge Amado was accused of essentially trafficking in worn-out stereotypes of Brazil and commercializing them for the world's consumption.

Paulo Coelho, on the other hand, cannot be accused of any such thing. One reason is that his books have almost no discernible trace of "brazilianness." The fairy-tale quality of his stories, especially *The Alchemist*, makes it very clear that historical accuracy is not the point of the story. In Coelho's case the arguments against him are of a different sort. First, there is the complaint that his Portuguese is, in fact, not very good. What is interesting is that most of his grammatical missteps are elided in translation. Thus, one only perceives them if one reads Portuguese, something that only a tiny portion of his readership does. In fact, these sins against grammar do nothing so much as give a mild colloquial quality to the language, and do not detract at all from the enjoyability and comprehensibility of the text. The complaint is more political than anything else, since Brazilian Portuguese, a language which still distinguishes sharply between written and spoken language, has also been open to the inclusion of colloquial speech in literature. The problem is political because it is understood that these inclusions were done by members of the intelligentsia whose intellectually elite status made them above reproach. Paulo Coelho was not part of this elite and his membership in the intellectual elite now is contentious.

One aspect of this contentiousness can be seen in reactions to Coelho's inclusion in the Brazilian Academy of Letters, the most prestigious group of literary intellectuals in Brazil. The Academy is a group of 40 poets and writers that meets every week and is a large intellectual force in Brazil. Paulo Coelho's acceptance into the Academy was an extremely controversial affair, in part because his work has been dubbed as sub-literary, as self-help literature, by much of the critical community. Even those who are not instantly repelled by the self-help theme of his books argue that what Coelho is espousing is a sort of religion stripped of all difficulty and hardship that is completely compatible with materialist consumerism. (Ironically, his proponents also point to these things as evidence of the vitality of his philosophy. Coelho indicates a completely pragmatic spirituality, they argue.) Detractors also point out the aforementioned use of Portuguese and the fact that Coelho's style does not warrant serious literary attention. These opinions are so commonplace that they have become something of a reflex in critical circles, prompting many to judge his novels without even reading them. A famous example is the printed remark of a critic for the Folha de Sao Paulo, a major national newspaper: "I didn't read it and I don't like it."

There are, however, proponents of Coelho's membership in the Academy and of his literature in general. Some claim that that his style is simplistic not because of any defect on his part, but because he is seeking to create a fairy-tale world whose depth comes not from the psychological complexity of the characters but from the message that it conveys to readers. On the other hand, there are plenty of proponents who would agree that Coelho's books are not of optimal quality nor are they great pieces of literature. What they are, though, are extremely important cultural artifacts. This is a man who has touched literally millions of lives using the written word. It also could be claimed that he is attracting readers that are in no way accustomed to reading or to literature in general. Thus, Paulo Coelho is doing Brazilian letters in particular a great service - by putting Brazil on the map as a center of relevant literature.

Paulo Coelho Photo

Photo of the author.

Author of ClassicNote and Sources

Anthony P. Arroyo, author of ClassicNote. Completed on December 01, 2008, copyright held by GradeSaver.

Updated and revised Damien Chazelle December 28, 2008. Copyright held by GradeSaver.

Paulo Coelho. The Alchemist. New York: Harper Collins, 1998.

Paulo Coelho. O Alquimista. Rio de Janeiro: Rocco, 1992.

Mário Maestri. Por que Paulo Coelho teve sucesso. Porto Alegre: AGE, 1999.

Janilto Andrade. Por que não ler Paulo Coelho. Rio de Janeiro: Calibán, 2004.

Alex Castro. "Paulo Coelho na Academia Brasileira de Letras." 2003-07-05. 2008-10-14. <http://www.sobresites.com/alexcastro/artigos/paulocoelho.htm>.

Paulo Coelho. "Official Site of Paulo Coelho." 2006-09-17. 2008-10-10. <http://www.paulocoelho.com.br/index.html>.

Paulo Coelho. "Interview with Paulo Coelho." 2008-10-21. <http://www.santjordi-asociados.com/interviews.htm>.

Quiz 1

1. **What region of Spain is Santiago from?**
   A. Galicia
   B. Tangiers
   C. Andalusia
   D. Tarifa

2. **What is the name of the wind that blows from Africa?**
   A. The Levantine
   B. Thurimm
   C. Umim
   D. The Levanter

3. **What is Santiago's original profession?**
   A. Sailor
   B. Goatherd
   C. Merchant
   D. Shepherd

4. **Melchizedek is the king of what kingdom?**
   A. Granada
   B. Sevilla
   C. Andalusia
   D. Salem

5. **How much treasure does the gypsy woman in Tarifa ask for?**
   A. One half
   B. One third
   C. One tenth
   D. One sixth

6. **How much of the flock does Melchizedek ask for?**
   A. One half
   B. One fifth
   C. One tenth
   D. One sixth

7. **What did Santiago do before shepherding?**
    A. Worked at a slaughter house
    B. Planted orange trees
    C. Attended the seminary
    D. Sold books

8. **Where does Santiago meet Melchizedek?**
    A. Sevilla
    B. Al-Fayoum
    C. Tangiers
    D. Tarifa

9. **What are the names of the black and white stones that Melchizedek gave to Santiago?**
    A. Black and White
    B. Urim and Thummim
    C. Urit and Thurrit
    D. Tundle and Dundle

10. **Where does Santiago disembark in Africa?**
    A. Granada
    B. Morocco
    C. Tangiers
    D. Tarifa

11. **What country is Al-Fayoum in?**
    A. Algeria
    B. Somalia
    C. Morocco
    D. Egypt

12. **What mythological character is the prologue about?**
    A. Oedipus
    B. Achilles
    C. Sisyphus
    D. Narcissus

13. **Why does the lake in the prologue weep?**
    A. Because it is in Greece
    B. Because it misses narcissus
    C. Because it doesn't have a Personal Legend
    D. Because it can't love

14. **What kind of tree is growing in the abandoned church where Santiago has his first dream?**
    A. Sycamore
    B. Oak
    C. Cedar
    D. Birch

15. **What are the only two things that Santiago's sheep worry about?**
    A. Food and water
    B. Wealth and power
    C. Shelter and procreating
    D. Fear and trembling

16. **How does Santiago meet the merchant's daughter?**
    A. He runs into her in the town square
    B. He sells her father some wool
    C. Melchizedek introduces them
    D. She reads his palm

17. **How did Santiago learn to read?**
    A. From being a merchant
    B. In the seminary
    C. From Melchizedek
    D. From a gypsy

18. **Why does Santiago leave the seminary?**
    A. Because he wants to become a Muslim
    B. Because he wants to find God on his own
    C. Because he doesn't believe in God
    D. Because he wants to travel

19. **Where does Santiago's father get the gold coins that he gives Santiago?**
    A. In a cave
    B. He found them in an abandoned church
    C. From his father
    D. In a field

20. **Besides his sheep and a jacket, what is the one thing that Santiago always carries while shepherding?**
    A. A cross
    B. A mirror
    C. A book
    D. A pipe

21. **Where does the dream interpreter live?**
    A. Algeria
    B. Sevilla
    C. Alhambra
    D. Tarifa

22. **In Santiago's dream, who shows him the treasure?**
    A. A woman
    B. An elf
    C. A camel
    D. A child

23. **In Santiago's dream, where is the treasure?**
    A. The Egyptian Pyramids
    B. Mt. Ararat
    C. Al-Fayoum
    D. The Pharoah's Tomb

24. **When Santiago swears to give the gypsy woman 1/10th of his treasure, what does he swear on?**
    A. A Relic of Santiago Matamoros
    B. The Bible
    C. The Sacred Heart of Jesus
    D. The Eye of God

25. **What is Santiago doing when he meets Melchizedek?**
    A. Reading a book
    B. Eating an apple
    C. Shearing a sheep
    D. Pondering his Personal Legend

Quiz 1 Answer Key

1. (C) Andalusia
2. (D) The Levanter
3. (D) Shepherd
4. (D) Salem
5. (C) One tenth
6. (C) One tenth
7. (C) Attended the seminary
8. (D) Tarifa
9. (B) Urim and Thummim
10. (C) Tangiers
11. (D) Egypt
12. (D) Narcissus
13. (B) Because it misses narcissus
14. (A) Sycamore
15. (A) Food and water
16. (B) He sells her father some wool
17. (B) In the seminary
18. (D) Because he wants to travel
19. (D) In a field
20. (C) A book
21. (D) Tarifa
22. (D) A child
23. (A) The Egyptian Pyramids
24. (C) The Sacred Heart of Jesus
25. (A) Reading a book

Quiz 2

1. **What does Melchizedek say is the world's greatest lie?**
    A. That gold can be made from lead
    B. That Egypt is dangerous
    C. That at some point, fate takes control of our lives and that it is out of
out hands
    D. That alchemists can live forever

2. **How does Melchizedek convince Santiago that he is not a fraud?**
    A. Melchizedek writes Santiago's whole life in the sand without being
told anything.
    B. Melchizedek turns water into wine
    C. Melchizedek makes the merchant's daughter fall in love with Santiago
    D. Melchizedek turns gold into lead

3. **What is a Personal Legend?**
    A. A spell which will give you the ability to live forever
    B. Your own secret history
    C. What you have always wanted to accomplish, even if you don't know
it
    D. A type of alchemist's spell

4. **What nourishes the Soul of the World?**
    A. Air
    B. Happiness
    C. Sand
    D. Water

5. **Why does Melchizedek appear to Santiago?**
    A. To warn him of his upcoming robbery
    B. To buy his sheep
    C. To help him realize his Personal Legend
    D. To warn him about the gypsy woman

6. **What else has Melchizedek appeared as, besides the King of Salem?**
    A. A broom
    B. A stone
    C. A baker
    D. A sheep

7. **What kind of payment does Melchizedek ask for from Santiago?**
   A. Jewels
   B. One tenth of his flock of sheep
   C. Gold
   D. A lock of hair

8. **What does Santiago do while pondering Melchizedek's offer?**
   A. Buys an ice-cream
   B. Drinks some wine
   C. Reads a book
   D. Walks to the ticket booth where they sell tickets to Africa

9. **What is Santiago's first good omen?**
   A. Buying a new book
   B. That it didn't rain
   C. That his friend bought his whole flock
   D. Finding an emerald

10. **What does Melchizedek wear under his cape?**
    A. A shirt
    B. Nothing
    C. Chain mail
    D. A gold breastplate

11. **In the story that Melchizedek tells Santiago, what does the wise man make the boy carry?**
    A. A stone
    B. Two stones
    C. A spoon full of oil
    D. A fork

12. **What did Santiago not count on before arriving in Africa?**
    A. That it was hot
    B. That he could not speak Arabic
    C. That he brought no clean clothes
    D. That he had no money

13. **What does Santiago drink in the first bar that he goes to in Tangiers?**
    A. Kombucha
    B. Tea
    C. Beer
    D. Wine

14. **Why doesn't the bar in Tangiers serve wine?**
    A. Beer is more common in Africa
    B. Too sweet
    C. Islam prohibits
    D. Prohibitively expensive

15. **When Santiago loses the boy in the market in Tangiers, what does he stop to look at?**
    A. A sword
    B. A snake charmer
    C. A wine jug
    D. A camel

16. **Where does Santiago sleep after being robbed in Tangiers?**
    A. The marketplace
    B. The church
    C. The mosque
    D. The bar

17. **When does Santiago use Urim and Thummim for the first time?**
    A. When washing his hands
    B. After arriving in Africa
    C. After being robbed in the market
    D. When deciding where to eat

18. **Who is the first person that helps Santiago after he has been robbed?**
    A. An imamm
    B. The candy seller
    C. A shepherd
    D. A young girl

19. **Where is the crystal shop in Tangiers located?**
    A. At the top of a hill
    B. On the waterfront
    C. By the river
    D. In the square

20. **What does Santiago offer to do when he walks into the crystal shop for the first time?**
    A. Make tea
    B. Sweep the floor
    C. Shear some sheep
    D. Clean the windows

21. **What does the Koran mandate the shopkeeper to do to hungry people?**
    A. Feed them
    B. Wash them
    C. House them
    D. Clothe them

22. **Initially, what does Santiago plan on doing with the money he saves from working at the crystal shop?**
    A. Buying some sheep and returning to Spain
    B. Buying some crystal
    C. Buying a camel
    D. Catching the thief from the market

23. **How long does Santiago work at the crystal shop?**
    A. One year
    B. Two years
    C. A few months
    D. Sixth months

24. **The shopkeeper calls the Pyramids nothing but...**
    A. A mound of dirt
    B. A pile of stones
    C. Relics of the past
    D. False idols

25. **To where does the shopkeeper want to make a pilgrimage?**
   A. Mecca
   B. Ceuta
   C. Egypt
   D. Tarifa

Quiz 2 Answer Key

1. **(C)** That at some point, fate takes control of our lives and that it is out of out hands
2. **(A)** Melchizedek writes Santiago's whole life in the sand without being told anything.
3. **(C)** What you have always wanted to accomplish, even if you don't know it
4. **(B)** Happiness
5. **(C)** To help him realize his Personal Legend
6. **(B)** A stone
7. **(B)** One tenth of his flock of sheep
8. **(D)** Walks to the ticket booth where they sell tickets to Africa
9. **(C)** That his friend bought his whole flock
10. **(D)** A gold breastplate
11. **(C)** A spoon full of oil
12. **(B)** That he could not speak Arabic
13. **(B)** Tea
14. **(C)** Islam prohibits
15. **(A)** A sword
16. **(A)** The marketplace
17. **(C)** After being robbed in the market
18. **(B)** The candy seller
19. **(A)** At the top of a hill
20. **(D)** Clean the windows
21. **(A)** Feed them
22. **(A)** Buying some sheep and returning to Spain
23. **(A)** One year
24. **(B)** A pile of stones
25. **(A)** Mecca

Quiz 3

1. **What are two improvements that Santiago makes to the crystal shop?**
    A. He builds two display cases
    B. He moves the shop and starts selling swords
    C. He starts selling beer and wine
    D. He builds a display case and starts selling tea

2. **What effect does Santiago have on business at the crystal shop?**
    A. It improves and then worsens
    B. No effect
    C. It worsens
    D. It improves

3. **What changes Santiago's mind about returning to Spain after working at the crystal shop?**
    A. Now that he had gotten by in Tangiers, he felt he could do anything
    B. Fear
    C. Love
    D. Lack of money

4. **Why does Santiago leave the crystal shop without saying good bye?**
    A. He is in a hurry
    B. Because he doesn't want to cry in front of customers
    C. He forgets to say good bye
    D. He and the shopkeeper had just quarreled

5. **How does Santiago know of the caravan across the desert?**
    A. The caravan supplies crystal to the shop
    B. The bartender recommends it
    C. The Englishman tells him
    D. He sees a sign

6. **Besides alchemy and religion, what did the Englishman study?**
    A. Chinese
    B. Esperanto
    C. Hindi
    D. Mathematics

7. **Why does the Englishman introduce himself to Santiago?**
    A. He doesn't
    B. They both speak English
    C. He recognizes Urim and Thummim
    D. They are wearing the same shirt

8. **Why is the Englishman headed to Al-Fayoum?**
    A. To find Fatima
    B. To find the Alchemist
    C. For fun and adventure
    D. He is a merchant

9. **Why does the Englishman want to buy Urim and Thummim?**
    A. Because he doesn't have a pair
    B. Because in England they are very expensive
    C. He doesn't
    D. Because they are very rare

10. **What is the universal language?**
    A. The language of omens
    B. Science
    C. Esperanto
    D. Math

11. **What does the caravan leader ask of the people in the caravan?**
    A. That they feed their camels
    B. That they swear allegiance to Allah
    C. That they give up their money
    D. That they follow his every order

12. **What impresses Santiago about the desert?**
    A. How small it is
    B. Its size and elemental force
    C. How fragile it is
    D. The variety of life in it

13. **What do the caravan leaders do if one them dies?**
    A. Eat his ration
    B. Give his clothes to the poor
    C. Marry his wife
    D. Draw lots and appoint a new one

14. **One of the camel drivers used to be a farmer in Egypt. Why did he become a camel driver?**
    A. He likes to travel the desert
    B. The Nile overflowed and destroyed his land
    C. The money
    D. The power

15. **What is the name of the people who bring news of war to the caravan?**
    A. Berbers
    B. Bedouins
    C. Eritreans
    D. Rikat

16. **What advice does Santiago give the Englishman in the desert?**
    A. To find some treasure
    B. To clean his gun
    C. To continue reading his books
    D. To learn from the desert

17. **Where is the secret of alchemy originally written?**
    A. The Orange Book
    B. The Diamond Slab
    C. The Emerald Tablet
    D. The Ruby Sun

18. **What is the liquid portion of the Master Work called?**
    A. The Elixir of Life
    B. Spark Fluid
    C. The Elixir of Power
    D. Emerald Brew

19. What is the solid portion of the Master Work called?
A. The Stone Abu Rai
B. The Philosopher's Stone
C. The Philodox's Rock
D. The Sorcerer's Stone

20. Why does Englishman claim the alchemy books are so complicated?
A. Their writers were possessed
B. Their writers were illiterate
C. To keep their secret safe
D. Their writers were blind

21. Why does Santiago respect the Englishman?
A. Because he speaks Esperanto
B. Because he is pursuing his Personal Legend
C. Because he is kind
D. Because he doesn't eat meat

22. In the opinion of the Alchemist, why do people forget the Language of the World?
A. They fall in love with words and pictures
B. They are greedy
C. They are stupid
D. They don't believe in Allah

23. Why don't invaders enter the oasis?
A. Because they can't find it
B. Because they are superstitious
C. Because oases are neutral
D. Because they don't have enough men

24. Why does the Englishman carry a revolver?
A. He doesn't
B. To rob travelers
C. It helps him to trust in people
D. To shoot game

25. **Where do the Englishman and Santiago go to ask people about the Alchemist?**
    A. The well
    B. The market
    C. The desert
    D. The mosque

Quiz 3 Answer Key

1. **(D)** He builds a display case and starts selling tea
2. **(D)** It improves
3. **(A)** Now that he had gotten by in Tangiers, he felt he could do anything
4. **(B)** Because he doesn't want to cry in front of customers
5. **(A)** The caravan supplies crystal to the shop
6. **(B)** Esperanto
7. **(C)** He recognizes Urim and Thummim
8. **(B)** To find the Alchemist
9. **(C)** He doesn't
10. **(A)** The language of omens
11. **(D)** That they follow his every order
12. **(B)** Its size and elemental force
13. **(D)** Draw lots and appoint a new one
14. **(B)** The Nile overflowed and destroyed his land
15. **(B)** Bedouins
16. **(D)** To learn from the desert
17. **(C)** The Emerald Tablet
18. **(A)** The Elixir of Life
19. **(B)** The Philosopher's Stone
20. **(C)** To keep their secret safe
21. **(B)** Because he is pursuing his Personal Legend
22. **(A)** They fall in love with words and pictures
23. **(C)** Because oases are neutral
24. **(C)** It helps him to trust in people
25. **(A)** The well

Quiz 4

1. **What is the name of the girl that Santiago falls in love with at Al-Fayoum?**
    A. Malia
    B. Fatima
    C. Sarifa
    D. Tarifa

2. **What kind of bird does Santiago observe fighting when he has his vision in the desert?**
    A. Falcons
    B. Sparrows
    C. Hawks
    D. Eagles

3. **What will Santiago receive for every ten foreigns fighter killed at Al-Fayoum?**
    A. An acre of land
    B. A piece of gold
    C. A piece of silver
    D. A sheep

4. **What is the name of the saint that Santiago references several time whose image is a white horse towering over infidels?**
    A. St. Agatha
    B. St. Lazarus
    C. St. Sebastian
    D. Santiago Matamoros

5. **Who is the main character of the story that the tribal elder at Al-Fayoum tells Santiago?**
    A. Sebastian of Memphis
    B. Joseph of Egypt
    C. Stephan of Cairo
    D. Ali of Mecca

6. **What is delaying Santiago's departure from the oasis?**
    A. He has run out of money
    B. The weather
    C. The war between the tribes
    D. No caravans go farther to the west

7. **Why does the alchemist recommend that Santiago buy a horse instead of a camel?**
   A. Horses die little by little
   B. Horses are more loyal
   C. Horses are more intelligent
   D. Horses are cheaper

8. **What kind of life does Santiago when asked by the alchemist?**
   A. A rabbit
   B. A scorpion
   C. A land shark
   D. A snake

9. **What is that only way to learn, according to the Alchemist?**
   A. By meditation
   B. By action
   C. By prayer
   D. By reading

10. **Why does the alchemist tell Santiago to listen to his heart?**
   A. Because Allah is the only God
   B. Because his heart never lies
   C. He doesn't
   D. Because his heart came from the Soul of the World

11. **What is worse than suffering, according to the Alchemist?**
   A. Being unhappy
   B. The fear of suffering
   C. Being poor
   D. Being lonely

12. **Besides the wind, the sun and the Soul of World, what else does Santiago ask to turn him into the wind?**
   A. The desert
   B. The clouds
   C. The plants
   D. The animals

13. **Where does Santiago go after he turns himself into the wind?**
    A. To the camel merchant
    B. To the jewel merchant
    C. Another village
    D. A Coptic monastery

14. **The Alchemist divides the gold he makes at the monastery four ways. How many part are for Santiago?**
    A. One
    B. Two
    C. None
    D. Three

15. **Why does the Alchemist leave some extra gold at the monastery?**
    A. As an offering
    B. In case Santiago needs it for the trip home
    C. He doesn't
    D. To bribe the monk

16. **Where is Santiago's treasure buried?**
    A. Ethiopia
    B. Spain
    C. Egypt
    D. France

17. **What kind of bird does the Alchemist carry on his shoulder?**
    A. A falcon
    B. A parrot
    C. A hawk
    D. A crow

18. **What happens when Santiago gets to the pyramids?**
    A. He has another vision
    B. He turns into the wind
    C. He is beaten and robbed
    D. He weeps for joy

19. **What does the robber tell Santiago at the pyramids?**
    A. That his dream was a lie
    B. That the robber had the same dream, but that the treasure is in Spain
    C. That he was a bad alchemist
    D. That alchemy is a lie

20. **What kind of beetle signals to Santiago that he should dig for the treasure?**
    A. A green beetle
    B. A scarab
    C. A fusca
    D. A black beetle

21. **Does the gypsy get her treasure in the end?**
    A. No
    B. Only half
    C. She can't be found
    D. Yes

22. **What country is Paulo Coelho from?**
    A. Brazil
    B. England
    C. Portugal
    D. France

23. **Where does Paulo Coelho live now?**
    A. New York
    B. France and Italy
    C. Brazil and Italy
    D. Brazil and France

24. **What was Coelho's profession prior to becoming a writer?**
    A. Mailman
    B. Lyricist
    C. Crystal merchant
    D. Love doctor

25. When was I[The Alchemist] originally published?
A. 1978
B. 1988
C. 1996
D. 2000

Quiz 4 Answer Key

1. **(B)** Fatima
2. **(C)** Hawks
3. **(B)** A piece of gold
4. **(D)** Santiago Matamoros
5. **(B)** Joseph of Egypt
6. **(C)** The war between the tribes
7. **(A)** Horses die little by little
8. **(D)** A snake
9. **(B)** By action
10. **(D)** Because his heart came from the Soul of the World
11. **(B)** The fear of suffering
12. **(A)** The desert
13. **(D)** A Coptic monastery
14. **(B)** Two
15. **(B)** In case Santiago needs it for the trip home
16. **(B)** Spain
17. **(A)** A falcon
18. **(C)** He is beaten and robbed
19. **(B)** That the robber had the same dream, but that the treasure is in Spain
20. **(B)** A scarab
21. **(D)** Yes
22. **(A)** Brazil
23. **(D)** Brazil and France
24. **(B)** Lyricist
25. **(B)** 1988

ClassicNotes

GradeSaver™

Getting you the grade since 1999™

Other ClassicNotes from GradeSaver™

1984
Absalom, Absalom
Adam Bede
The Adventures of Augie
    March
The Adventures of
    Huckleberry Finn
The Adventures of Tom
    Sawyer
The Aeneid
Agamemnon
The Age of Innocence
The Alchemist (Coelho)
The Alchemist (Jonson)
Alice in Wonderland
All My Sons
All Quiet on the Western
    Front
All the King's Men
All the Pretty Horses
Allen Ginsberg's Poetry
The Ambassadors
American Beauty
And Then There Were
    None
Angela's Ashes
Animal Farm
Anna Karenina
Anthem
Antigone
Antony and Cleopatra
Aristotle's Ethics
Aristotle's Poetics
Aristotle's Politics
As I Lay Dying
As You Like It

Astrophil and Stella
Atlas Shrugged
Atonement
The Awakening
Babbitt
The Bacchae
Bartleby the Scrivener
The Bean Trees
The Bell Jar
Beloved
Benito Cereno
Beowulf
Bhagavad-Gita
Billy Budd
Black Boy
Bleak House
Bless Me, Ultima
Blindness
Blood Wedding
The Bloody Chamber
Bluest Eye
The Bonfire of the
    Vanities
The Book of the Duchess
    and Other Poems
The Book Thief
Brave New World
Breakfast at Tiffany's
Breakfast of Champions
The Brief Wondrous Life
    of Oscar Wao
The Brothers Karamazov
The Burning Plain and
    Other Stories
A Burnt-Out Case
By Night in Chile

Call of the Wild
Candide
The Canterbury Tales
Cat on a Hot Tin Roof
Cat's Cradle
Catch-22
The Catcher in the Rye
The Caucasian Chalk
    Circle
Charlotte Temple
Charlotte's Web
The Cherry Orchard
The Chocolate War
The Chosen
A Christmas Carol
Christopher Marlowe's
    Poems
Chronicle of a Death
    Foretold
Civil Disobedience
Civilization and Its
    Discontents
A Clockwork Orange
Coleridge's Poems
The Color of Water
The Color Purple
Comedy of Errors
Communist Manifesto
A Confederacy of
    Dunces
Confessions
Connecticut Yankee in
    King Arthur's Court
The Consolation of
    Philosophy
Coriolanus

For our full list of over 250 Study Guides, Quizzes,
Sample College Application Essays, Literature Essays and E-texts, visit:

www.gradesaver.com

ClassicNotes

GradeSaver™

Getting you the grade since 1999™

Other ClassicNotes from GradeSaver™

The Count of Monte
   Cristo
The Country Wife
Crime and Punishment
The Crucible
Cry, the Beloved
   Country
The Crying of Lot 49
The Curious Incident of
   the Dog in the
   Night-time
Cymbeline
Daisy Miller
David Copperfield
Death in Venice
Death of a Salesman
The Death of Ivan Ilych
Democracy in America
Devil in a Blue Dress
Dharma Bums
The Diary of a Young
   Girl by Anne Frank
Disgrace
Divine Comedy-I:
   Inferno
Do Androids Dream of
   Electric Sheep?
Doctor Faustus
   (Marlowe)
A Doll's House
Don Quixote Book I
Don Quixote Book II
Dora: An Analysis of a
   Case of Hysteria
Dr. Jekyll and Mr. Hyde
Dracula

Dubliners
East of Eden
Electra by Sophocles
The Electric Kool-Aid
   Acid Test
Emily Dickinson's
   Collected Poems
Emma
Ender's Game
Endgame
The English Patient
The Epic of Gilgamesh
Ethan Frome
The Eumenides
Everyman: Morality Play
Everything is Illuminated
The Faerie Queene
Fahrenheit 451
The Fall of the House of
   Usher
A Farewell to Arms
The Federalist Papers
Fences
Flags of Our Fathers
Flannery O'Connor's
   Stories
For Whom the Bell Tolls
The Fountainhead
Frankenstein
Franny and Zooey
The Giver
The Glass Castle
The Glass Menagerie
The God of Small Things
Goethe's Faust
The Good Earth

The Good Woman of
   Setzuan
The Grapes of Wrath
Great Expectations
The Great Gatsby
Grendel
The Guest
Gulliver's Travels
Hamlet
The Handmaid's Tale
Hard Times
Haroun and the Sea of
   Stories
Harry Potter and the
   Philosopher's Stone
Heart of Darkness
Hedda Gabler
Henry IV (Pirandello)
Henry IV Part 1
Henry IV Part 2
Henry V
Herzog
Hippolytus
The Hobbit
Homo Faber
House of Mirth
The House of the Seven
   Gables
The House of the Spirits
House on Mango Street
How the Garcia Girls
   Lost Their Accents
Howards End
A Hunger Artist
I Know Why the Caged
   Bird Sings

For our full list of over 250 Study Guides, Quizzes,
Sample College Application Essays, Literature Essays and E-texts, visit:

www.gradesaver.com

ClassicNotes

GradeSaver™

Getting you the grade since 1999™

Other ClassicNotes from GradeSaver™

Northanger Abbey
Notes from Underground
O Pioneers
The Odyssey
Oedipus Rex or Oedipus the King
Of Mice and Men
The Old Man and the Sea
Oliver Twist
On Liberty
On the Road
One Day in the Life of Ivan Denisovich
One Flew Over the Cuckoo's Nest
One Hundred Years of Solitude
Oroonoko
Oryx and Crake
Othello
Our Town
The Outsiders
Pale Fire
Pamela: Or Virtue Rewarded
Paradise Lost
A Passage to India
The Pearl
Percy Shelley: Poems
Perfume: The Story of a Murderer
Persepolis: The Story of a Childhood
Persuasion
Phaedra
Phaedrus

The Piano Lesson
The Picture of Dorian Gray
Poe's Poetry
Poe's Short Stories
Poems of W.B. Yeats: The Rose
Poems of W.B. Yeats: The Tower
The Poems of William Blake
The Poetry of Robert Frost
The Poisonwood Bible
Pope's Poems and Prose
Portrait of the Artist as a Young Man
Pride and Prejudice
The Prince
The Professor's House
Prometheus Bound
Pudd'nhead Wilson
Pygmalion
Rabbit, Run
A Raisin in the Sun
The Real Life of Sebastian Knight
Rebecca
The Red Badge of Courage
The Remains of the Day
The Republic
Rhinoceros
Richard II
Richard III

The Rime of the Ancient Mariner
Rip Van Winkle and Other Stories
The Road
Robinson Crusoe
Roll of Thunder, Hear My Cry
Romeo and Juliet
A Room of One's Own
A Room With a View
A Rose For Emily and Other Short Stories
Rosencrantz and Guildenstern Are Dead
Salome
The Scarlet Letter
The Scarlet Pimpernel
The Seagull
Season of Migration to the North
Second Treatise of Government
The Secret Life of Bees
The Secret River
Secret Sharer
Sense and Sensibility
A Separate Peace
Shakespeare's Sonnets
Shantaram
Short Stories of Ernest Hemingway
Short Stories of F. Scott Fitzgerald
Siddhartha

For our full list of over 250 Study Guides, Quizzes,
Sample College Application Essays, Literature Essays and E-texts, visit:

www.gradesaver.com

ClassicNotes

GradeSaver™

Getting you the grade since 1999™

Other ClassicNotes from GradeSaver™

Silas Marner
Sir Gawain and the
    Green Knight
Sister Carrie
Six Characters in Search
    of an Author
Slaughterhouse Five
Snow Falling on Cedars
The Social Contract
Something Wicked This
    Way Comes
Song of Roland
Song of Solomon
Songs of Innocence and
    of Experience
Sons and Lovers
The Sorrows of Young
    Werther
The Sound and the Fury
The Spanish Tragedy
Spenser's Amoretti and
    Epithalamion
Spring Awakening
The Stranger
A Streetcar Named
    Desire
Sula
The Sun Also Rises
Tale of Two Cities
The Taming of the Shrew
The Tempest
Tender is the Night
Tess of the D'Urbervilles
Their Eyes Were
    Watching God
Things Fall Apart

The Things They Carried
A Thousand Splendid
    Suns
The Threepenny Opera
Through the Looking
    Glass
Thus Spoke Zarathustra
The Time Machine
Titus Andronicus
To Build a Fire
To Kill a Mockingbird
To the Lighthouse
The Tortilla Curtain
Touching Spirit Bear
Treasure Island
Trifles
Troilus and Cressida
Tropic of Cancer
Tropic of Capricorn
Tuesdays With Morrie
The Turn of the Screw
Twelfth Night
Twilight
Ulysses
Uncle Tom's Cabin
Utopia
Vanity Fair
A Very Old Man With
    Enormous Wings
Villette
The Visit
Volpone
Waiting for Godot
Waiting for Lefty
Walden
Washington Square

The Waste Land
The Wealth of Nations
Where the Red Fern
    Grows
White Fang
A White Heron and
    Other Stories
White Noise
White Teeth
Who's Afraid of Virginia
    Woolf
Wide Sargasso Sea
Wieland
Winesburg, Ohio
The Winter's Tale
The Woman Warrior
Wordsworth's Poetical
    Works
Woyzeck
A Wrinkle in Time
Wuthering Heights
The Yellow Wallpaper
Yonnondio: From the
    Thirties
Zeitoun

For our full list of over 250 Study Guides, Quizzes,
Sample College Application Essays, Literature Essays and E-texts, visit:

www.gradesaver.com

Made in the USA
Monee, IL
06 October 2024

67183209R00056